Abu

Abu is a mischievous little monkey and Aladdin's oldest friend. The two buddies help each other out while living on the streets of Agrabah. Even though Abu's monkey business sometimes gets Aladdin into trouble, Aladdin still loves his furry pal!

Abu's small size and lightning-fast paws make him a great ally if you're in trouble. When Jafar betrays Aladdin and tries to take the Genie's lamp for himself, Abu's sticky fingers help him grab the lamp without Jafar noticing.

FUN FACT

The actor who provided the voice of Abu also plays Jasmine's tiger friend, Rajah!

Abu's sticky fingers can come in handy sometimes!

Aladdin

Just be yourself. That's exactly what Aladdin learns . . . even though it takes him a while to figure it out!

At first, when Aladdin meets Jasmine on the street, he doesn't know that she is the Sultan's daughter—or that she is running away from a bunch of suitors who want to marry her. She just wants a simple life, while Aladdin dreams of what it would be like to live in a palace.

Later, when he learns who Jasmine really is, he tries to impress her by pretending to be a prince. Oops—big mistake! Jasmine just wants Aladdin to be himself. Only when Aladdin finally stops pretending does Jasmine truly fall for him.

Aladdin's high-flying skills help him escape from the palace guards.

TRICKY TRIVIA

Q: What name does Aladdin use when he disguises himself as a prince?

A: Prince Ali Ababwa

Alice

Poor Alice! All she wants is to have an adventure, instead of listening to her sister read history books. But when she follows the White Rabbit (simply out of curiosity), she tumbles down a deep hole and ends up in Wonderland. As Alice tries to find her way home, she meets many strange creatures who seem to enjoy mocking her, teasing her, or making her solve tricky riddles! But when the Queen of Hearts threatens to chop off her head, Alice takes matters into her own hands, and escapes back home. After her upsetting adventure, Alice is more than happy to listen to a few dull history books!

DID YOU KNOW?

When Alice plays croquet with the Queen of Hearts, they use flamingos as mallets and hedgehogs as balls.

Alice meets the Mad Hatter and the March Hare at a very unusual tea party.

Anastasia & Drizella

Cinderella's two nasty stepsisters are just plain mean. They make Cinderella wait on them all the time, and when Cinderella does get a chance to enjoy something, they do their best to ruin it for her. But these spoiled sisters are really just jealous of the kind and optimistic Cinderella.

Anastasia and Drizella both try to wear the glass slipper—but it only fits Cinderella!

TRICKY TRIVIA

Q: Do you know which sister is Anastasia and which is Drizella?

A: Anastasia has red hair and bangs. Drizella has brown hair, parted down the middle.

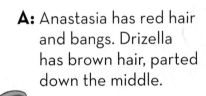

Anna

When Anna was a little girl, she and her sister, Elsa, were the best of friends. Anna was one of the only people who knew about Elsa's gift: Elsa has the power to make ice and snow with just her hands! But one day, Elsa's powers accidentally hurt Anna. After that, Elsa stayed away from Anna, hoping to protect her. But now, after many adventures, Anna and Elsa are best friends again.

Anna grew up to be a fearless optimist. She believes anything is possible if you have the courage to try. And she's fine as long as her family is happy, as long as Arendelle is safe, and as long as she never has to be alone again.

Anna promises never to leave Olaf . . . "not ever."

COOL QUOTE

"I don't think Olaf should get to rearrange."

Ariel

As a mermaid, Ariel longs for adventure and romance . . . and to visit the human world. To help her dreams come true, Ariel makes a bargain with the wicked sea witch, Ursula. She risks everything—not just her beautiful mermaid voice, but also (unbeknownst to her) her father's reign over Atlantica—to have three days on land as a human.

But when her deal with Ursula goes awry, Ariel must pull off some heroic feats to save Atlantica from the sea witch. She also wins the heart of Prince Eric and convinces her father to allow her to stay on land as a human. Now Ariel is part of the world she always dreamed of.

Ariel tests out her brand-new toes!

TRICKY TRIVIA

Q: How old is Ariel in *The Little Mermaid*?

A: Sixteen

Art

Art is a little . . . odd. None of the other students at Monsters University really know much about his past. But that doesn't stop the monsters of Oozma Kappa from accepting him! Along with the other members of his monstrous fraternity, Art competes in the Scare Games to win a place in the Scaring Program.

Art's interest in the unknown led him to become a new age philosophy major. He keeps a dream journal of all his crazy nightmares and doesn't work out because he doesn't want to "get too big." All in all, Art is up for anything, and his positive outlook on life is heartfelt, if a little wacky.

COOL QUOTES

"I just want a piece of the action!"

"Of all the sewers on campus, this one has always been my favorite."

"I have an extra toe. Not with me, of course. . . ."

Ta-da!

Atta

Princess Atta is one worried bug. As future leader of the anthill, Atta wants to be prepared for anything that could possibly go wrong. And when you're friends with bumbling inventor Flik, things seem to go wrong an awful lot!

Atta wants to take good care of all her ant subjects. After Hopper and his grasshoppers threaten the anthill, she and Flik team up to drive the pesky insects away forever.

Atta isn't sure what to make of Flik's new invention!

FUN FACT

Atta, the Queen, and Princess Dot are the only ants in the anthill who can fly. That's because only royal ants have wings!

Aurora

As a baby, Princess Aurora received three good blessings and one terrible curse. The three good fairies give her the gifts of song, beauty . . . and a way to reverse Maleficent's curse (that the girl will prick her finger on a spinning wheel and die before her sixteenth birthday). Still, Maleficent's words are frightening to all who love the tiny princess. As a result, the good fairies take Aurora deep into the woods, where they raise her in secrecy. She lives happily as a peasant girl and has no idea that she is a princess. Then, on the day of her sixteenth birthday, she returns to the castle, pricks her finger, and falls into a deep sleep.

Fortunately, her one true love, Prince Phillip, is able to defeat Maleficent and awaken Aurora with True Love's Kiss. Now free of the curse, Aurora can live a life of love and happiness as a true princess.

When Aurora meets Prince Phillip in the woods, it's love at first sight!

TRICKY TRIVIA

Q: What do the good fairies name Aurora to hide her true identity?

A: Briar Rose

Bagheera & Baloo

These jungle friends couldn't be more different! Bagheera is serious and a bit of a worrywart. Plus, he has a tough time keeping Baloo the bear in line! But Bagheera only tries to stop the fun and games because he wants to keep Mowgli safe.

Baloo is easygoing and lovable. He believes in living by the bare necessities and not sweating the big stuff. But when it comes to Mowgli's well-being, Baloo is just as protective as his panther friend.

With two great friends looking out for him, Mowgli couldn't be better off!

Sometimes Baloo drives Bagheera crazy!

DID YOU KNOW?

Baloo and *Bagheera* are Hindi words for "bear" and "panther."

Bambi

When Bambi the fawn is born, the forest comes alive with excitement. "The young prince is born!" rabbits and skunks and birds cry as they visit Bambi for the first time.

Bambi really is a prince. His father, a noble buck, is the Great Prince of the Forest.

Bambi's parents teach him all about the forest, the seasons, how to get food, and how to one day take his father's place as leader of the woodlands.

Bambi makes some new friends.

FUN FACT

The animators at the Disney studios wanted to make sure Bambi acted like a real deer. To help them out, live deer were brought into the studios so that the animators could study how they look and move.

Barley Lightfoot

Barley Lightfoot is a burly nineteen-year-old elf who believes there is still magic in the modern-day world. He is more interested in playing his favorite game, *Quests of Yore*, or embarking on real quests in his beloved beat-up old van, Guinevere, than in dealing with real-world problems. Fun, loud, devoted, and loyal, Barley will do anything for his friends and family. More than anything else, he loves and encourages his brother, Ian, in ways that are as uplifting as they are irritating. Barley's unique understanding of magic and quests is a very helpful resource once he and Ian embark on the adventure of a lifetime.

Barley loves giving his little brother, Ian, a playful noogie.

COOL QUOTE

"Uh, *Quests of Yore* isn't just a board game, it's a historically based role-playing scenario. Did you know in the old days centaurs could run seventy miles an hour?"

Basil of Baker Street

Even though he seems an awful lot like the great detective Sherlock Holmes, Basil is really a tiny mouse. Brilliant and determined to help little Olivia Flaversham find her father, Basil also wants to beat his rival, the evil Professor Ratigan. Impressed with his own cleverness, Basil goes about his business with the bumbling and lovable Dr. Dawson by his side. And in the end, Basil triumphs—not only by rescuing Olivia and her father but also by beating mean old Ratigan once and for all.

Time's up for Basil!

FUN FACT

Basil's address is 221½ Baker Street (the basement section).

The Beast

Once, as a young prince, he cruelly refused to give shelter to a peddler woman on a snowy night. Big mistake! The woman was an enchantress in disguise, and as punishment, she transformed him into a monstrous beast. Now the Beast has to learn to love and be loved before the last petal falls from a magical rose. If he does, he will become human again. But the Beast is convinced no one could ever love him.

When Belle comes to stay at his castle, the Beast has hope for the first time in years. Eventually, he not only earns Belle's love but also learns to show his kindness, courage, and patience. Then the spell is broken, and the Beast transforms into a human being once again.

Belle brings out the Beast's soft side.

FUN FACT

The Beast has a bear's body, a lion's mane, a buffalo's head, a boar's tusks, and a wolf's tail and legs!

Belle

Belle has always wanted to have an adventure. That's why she loves books so much—they can take her on imaginary adventures to exciting faraway lands. But Belle discovers real-life adventures are a lot different than she expected.

When Belle meets the Beast, she thinks he is horrible and cruel for imprisoning her father. Courageously, she convinces the Beast to let her trade places with her father and stay at the Beast's castle. Soon she finds a kind heart beneath the Beast's gruff exterior. By falling in love, she breaks the Beast's enchantment, and the two live happily ever after.

FUN FACT

Belle is the only character in her village who wears the color blue. The animators thought that would emphasize how different and out of place she is there.

Bookworm Belle

Bernard & Bianca

These two mice are members of the Rescue Aid Society—an elite group of mice dedicated to helping others. When Bianca is sent on a mission to recue an orphan named Penny, she has her pick of any companion, and she chooses the bumbling but lovable Bernard. Though much less adventurous than the glamorous Bianca, Bernard nevertheless takes his assignment very seriously: what could be more important than rescuing a little orphan girl? During their mission, Bernard wins Bianca's heart— simply by allowing her to see the goodness of his own.

Evinrude takes Bianca and Bernard on a wild ride!

TRICKY TRIVIA

Q: Who flies Bernard and Bianca to find Penny?

A: Orville

Q: Which country is Bianca from?

A: Hungary

The Blue Fairy

Though she has a small role in the film *Pinocchio*, the Blue Fairy makes a big difference for the little puppet. First of all, she assigns Jiminy Cricket as Pinocchio's conscience. Although the little cricket has a hard time keeping Pinocchio out of trouble, he does his best to keep him on the straight and narrow. The Blue Fairy can also tell when Pinocchio is lying. His nose grows into a rather long tree branch as he fibs! Finally, it is the Blue Fairy who deems Pinocchio to be good—good enough, in fact, for her to turn him from a puppet into a real boy.

The Blue Fairy brings Pinocchio to life.

COOL QUOTE

"You may be a real boy someday, but first you must prove yourself brave, truthful, and unselfish. You must learn to choose between right and wrong."

Boo

Boo first meets Sulley when she accidentally goes through her closet door and ends up in Monstropolis. At first, the big, scary monster is terrified of *her*. Like all monsters, Sulley thinks human children are highly toxic. Not knowing what else to do, Sulley tries to hide her from the other monsters. But Boo's adorable antics soon win over Sulley and his best friend, Mike. So much so that the two are willing to risk everything in order to return her safely home.

Sulley sneaks Boo into Monsters, Inc., with a disguise.

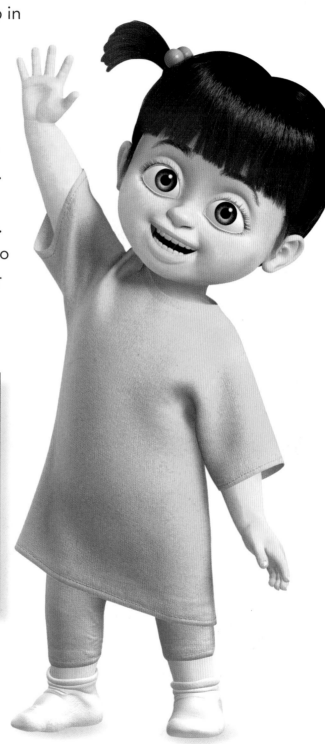

TRICKY TRIVIA

Q: What is Boo's nickname for Sulley?

A: Kitty

Bo Peep

Bo Peep, a porcelain figurine, was the leader of Andy's little sister's room until Molly outgrew her and gave her away. After serving a stint in an antiques store, Bo set out on her own with her sheep and her new friend Giggle in tow. But when Woody comes back into her life, she finds herself confronting her past and wondering if there could be more meaning in her future.

Bo Peep agrees to help Woody rescue Forky.

COOL QUOTE

"I didn't want to sit on a shelf waiting for my life to happen. So I left."

Buzz Lightyear

When Andy gets the one toy he really wants for his birthday—Buzz Lightyear—it sends the rest of Andy's toys into a panic. They are all worried that they will be thrown away or forgotten when this newer, shinier toy enters their little world. But Buzz Lightyear is most threatening to Woody, who has been Andy's favorite toy until now.

Eventually, though, the rivalry between Woody and Buzz turns into a true friendship, and they have lots of adventures together. Now the toys are friends for life!

Ducky and Bunny try to chase Buzz but get stuck!

COOL QUOTES

"To infinity . . . and beyond!"

"Good work, Inner Voice."

25

Captain Hook

Captain Hook, though a villainous pirate, is really quite cowardly. He often has to call for help from his trusty friend Smee. Hook's number-one goal is revenge on Peter Pan, who once cut off the pirate's left hand and fed it to a crocodile.

Hook is determined to find Peter's hideout and is always coming up with schemes to trap Peter—like kidnapping Tiger Lily. Unfortunately for the old "codfish," his devious plans are never successful, and he's constantly outwitted by Peter. Plus, Peter always manages to embarrass Hook in the process!

Captain Hook leaves a "gift" for Peter.

TRICKY TRIVIA

Q: What is Captain Hook's first name?

A: James

Carl Fredricksen

Carl Fredricksen once dreamed of being an adventurer and traveling all around the world. But at seventy-eight years old, he had started to feel as if life had passed him by. Carl still had one dream, however: to fly his house to Paradise Falls, in honor of his late wife, Ellie. With the help of a young boy named Russell, Carl makes that dream come true—and, along the way, finds a new dream to live for.

Dug and Russell hug it out.

TRICKY TRIVIA

Q: As a child, Carl dreamed he'd grow up to be an explorer. But what did he really become?

A: A balloon salesman

Chip & Dale

Chip and Dale are two little chipmunks with two big personalities. Chip is more responsible and no-nonsense, while Dale is a bit more scatterbrained and easygoing. They are always trying to gather a great stockpile of acorns . . . and if they can tease their friends Donald Duck and Pluto in the process, all the better!

DID YOU KNOW?

It's easy to tell the chipmunks apart:

Chip has a small black nose and one buck tooth.

Dale has a big red nose and two gap teeth.

Chip and Dale enjoy dinner—straight from Donald's kitchen!

Cinderella

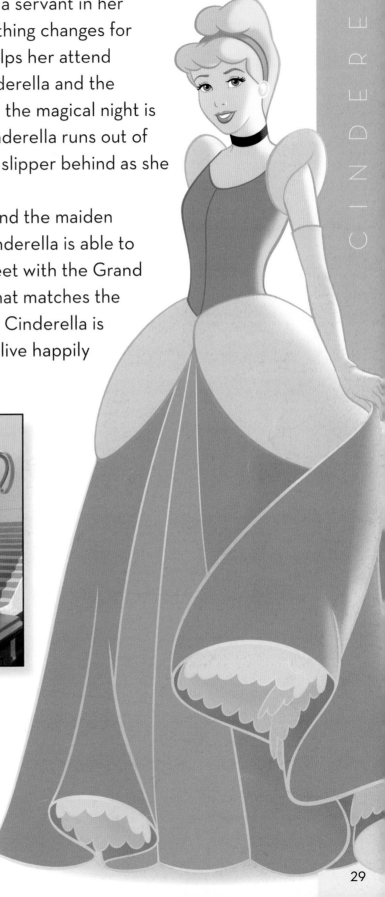

Cinderella wakes up every morning as a servant in her own home. But one magical night, everything changes for Cinderella when her fairy godmother helps her attend Prince Charming's royal ball. There Cinderella and the Prince fall in love. All too soon, however, the magical night is over. The clock strikes midnight, and Cinderella runs out of the castle, accidentally leaving her glass slipper behind as she returns home.

The Prince sends his grand duke to find the maiden whose foot fits into the glass slipper. Cinderella is able to overcome her wicked stepfamily and meet with the Grand Duke. She shows him the glass slipper that matches the one she left behind on the palace steps. Cinderella is soon reunited with the Prince, and they live happily ever after.

Cinderella is in quite a hurry!

FUN FACT

When Cinderella dances— and falls in love—with Prince Charming, she doesn't even realize he's the Prince!

Colette

Colette is the only female chef at Gusteau's restaurant—and the toughest one, as well. Her skills with a knife are as fast and sharp as her tongue. At first, she's annoyed at being assigned to "babysit" Linguini when he starts working in the kitchen at Gusteau's. But before long, even Colette can't help enjoying her time coaching him. After Linguini is fired from Gusteau's, she even quits to work with him at his new restaurant.

Colette takes a listen to a fresh loaf.

COOL QUOTE

"How do you tell great bread without tasting it? The sound!"

Cruella De Vil

Cruella De Vil is obsessed with fur. "I live for fur!" The "devil woman" goes as far as stealing Dalmatian puppies so that she can make a coat out of their spotted fur. Luckily, the clever little puppies have lots of dog friends and family members—as well as their own wits—to help them get out of Cruella's wicked grasp.

Don't drive like Cruella!

DID YOU KNOW?

Cruella De Vil's name is a play on the words *cruel* and *devil*.

Crush & Squirt

Thanks to this laid-back father-and-son pair, Marlin and Dory make it to safety after their dangerous jellyfish encounter. Leading by example, Crush and Squirt also teach Marlin a little about parenting. When Squirt swims out into the mighty East Australian Current, Crush lets him go—something Marlin would never let Nemo do! Impressed, Marlin asks Crush how he knows when a child is ready to go out on their own, and the turtle coolly replies, "Well, you never really know. But when they know, you'll know. You know?"

Crush and Squirt love to ride the EAC.

COOL QUOTES

"No hurlin' on the shell, okay? Just waxed it."—Crush

"You rock, dude!" —Squirt

32

Cruz Ramirez

Cruz Ramirez is a top-notch trainer at the Rust-eze Racing Center, where she's assigned to train the team's talented rookies. Her unconventional training methods have helped many young Piston Cup racers meet their goals on the track. Cruz once had racing dreams of her own, but it isn't until she meets Lightning McQueen that she realizes her passion to compete is still there. Now she'll finally get the chance to see if she has what it takes to win.

Lightning and Cruz get muddy at the demolition derby!

DID YOU KNOW?

Cruz's nickname is the Maestro of Motivation.

Daisy Duck

Daisy Duck is romantic, sophisticated, modern, and sometimes temperamental, especially when she has to deal with her boyfriend, Donald Duck. She can be a demanding girlfriend at times, but she is also enthusiastic and very much in love with Donald. Daisy loves shopping, having fun with her friends, and spending as much time as she can with her best friend, Minnie Mouse.

Daisy bakes cupcakes with her BFF, Minnie.

TRICKY TRIVIA

Q: What are the names of Daisy's three nieces?

A: April, May, and June

Donald Duck

Donald is one hot-tempered fella with a heart of gold. He always seems to be getting into some kind of trouble. Donald gets angry and frustrated, but he is also brave, determined, stubborn, and he would do anything for his family. He is lazy but inventive, and he always starts a new adventure with much optimism and enthusiasm. He's great pals with Mickey Mouse, and Daisy Duck will always be his sweetheart.

"Wak!"

COOL QUOTE
"Oh, boy! Oh, boy! Oh, boy!"

Dory

You'll never meet a fish friendlier, more hospitable, or more sociable than Dory. She'd love to chat with you all day and tell you her life story . . . though unfortunately, because she suffers from severe short-term memory loss, she can't. But that doesn't stop her from helping a clownfish named Marlin on his journey to find his son, Nemo, and her enduring optimism plays no small part in his success. Dory's positive attitude keeps Marlin going, even when things look hopeless. Marlin does eventually find his son, and Dory finds a new home with Marlin and Nemo.

"Hey, Mr. Grumpy Gills!"

COOL QUOTES

"I shall call him Squishy and he shall be mine and he shall be my Squishy."

"Wow. I wish I could speak whale."

"Just keep swimming."

Ducky & Bunny

Carnival prizes Ducky and Bunny have always been together—literally. They hang together from the ceiling of a carnival game booth, so they are a little tired of each other's company. But what Ducky and Bunny want more than anything is a kid of their own. They have seen so many toys come and go from their booth, and they hope their turn will come soon. Then one day, they are knocked from their perch by none other than Buzz Lightyear, sending them on a big adventure through the carnival and beyond.

Buzz is stuck on the game wall with Ducky and Bunny.

COOL QUOTE

"This is what I've been talking about, Bunny. You need to work on paying attention and your listening skills."

Dumbo

FUN FACT

Dumbo doesn't speak throughout the entire film.

When Dumbo is first delivered via stork to Mrs. Jumbo, the baby elephant seems perfect in every way . . . until he sneezes and reveals his giant ears. Luckily, Dumbo's mother loves her son just the way he is.

Then one terrible day, a mean boy mocks Dumbo. When Mrs. Jumbo defends her son, she ends up in jail—everyone thinks she's a crazy and dangerous elephant. Dumbo is heartbroken and misses his mother terribly. But soon he is befriended by the kindhearted and circus-savvy Timothy Mouse, who helps Dumbo gain confidence in himself. In the end, Dumbo's ears prove to be truly extraordinary— they help him to fly! This brings little Dumbo fame and fortune, but most importantly, it reunites him with his beloved mother.

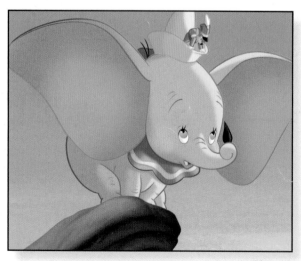

"You're standing on the threshold of success!"

Edna Mode

Brilliant and successful, Edna Mode got her start in the fashion industry as the world's leading costume designer for the Supers. Of course, once the Supers had to go into hiding, she took her talents to the world of high-end fashion and soon became the top name in design. Edna's passion, however, will always be combining the latest in textile technology with her impeccable sense of style to create the world's most incredible—and wearable—Supersuits. She even creates a special suit to help baby Jack-Jack control his newfound powers.

Edna likes babysitting Jack-Jack!

COOL QUOTES

"I never look back, dahling. It distracts from the now."

"No capes!"

Eeyore

"Looks like rain." Or at least that's what Eeyore would say (even on a sunny day). Eeyore is so gloomy he speaks in a deep monotone and hardly has the energy to form complete sentences. Still, Eeyore is a good friend and will do practically anything to help out his pals in the Hundred-Acre Wood.

COOL QUOTES

"Thanks for noticing."

"It's not much of a tail, but I'm sort of attached to it."

"Good morning. If it is a good morning, which I doubt."

When Eeyore loses his tail, his friends try to help him find a replacement— like a bright red balloon!

Elastigirl

Adjusting to "normal" life was no problem for Elastigirl (aka Helen Parr) when the government forced the Supers to go into hiding. After all, raising three kids and running a household can keep a person pretty busy. But when her family's safety is threatened, Elastigirl jumps at the chance to get back into full Super mode and come to the rescue. Eventually, she is able to apprehend the villainous Evelyn and restore legal status to all Supers around the world!

COOL QUOTE

"Leave the saving of the world to the men? I don't think so!"

Elastigirl and Evelyn fall out of a jet toward the sea.

Elsa

Elsa is poised, regal, and reserved. It would be hard for someone who had just met her to believe that Elsa used to hide under that exterior, encased in a world of fear, terrified that people would find out about her powers of ice and snow. But once Anna helped her embrace who she was and let go of that fear, she was able to shed the world of isolation she had locked herself in. Deep down, Elsa can't help wondering why she was born with such powers—powers that have grown over the years and continue to evolve.

The Wind Spirit sends Anna, Elsa, and their friends swirling up high!

COOL QUOTE

"Mother, do you think Ahtohallan knows why I have powers?"

Eric

Eric may be a prince, but he still loves a hard day's work sailing at sea. He even decides to celebrate his eighteenth birthday aboard his ship, rather than in his fancy palace. But disaster strikes the party when the ship gets caught in a terrible storm. Fortunately, the mermaid Ariel saves the prince's life—and he falls in love with her. Not so fortunately, when he meets Ariel again as a human, he doesn't recognize her! But even though she may look a little different, the pair fall in love all over again. Eric and Ariel even fight the evil sea witch Ursula together to save their kingdoms. Once both land and sea are safe, the two can finally be together.

Kiss the girl!

TRICKY TRIVIA

Q: What is the name of Eric's dog?

A: Max

EVE

Pure white, egg-shaped, graceful—and fully armed!—EVE is by far the most beautiful thing WALL•E has ever seen when she lands on his trash-filled planet. WALL•E wants nothing more than to hold her "hand," but EVE is on a mission to scout out living plant life on Earth. She wants to know if the planet can support human life. When she finds a plant (thanks to WALL•E), nothing stops her from accomplishing her directive. She soon discovers, though, how valuable friendship can be.

EVE defends her robot friends from the *Axiom*'s evil autopilot.

TRICKY TRIVIA

Q: What does "EVE" stand for?

A: Extra-terrestrial Vegetation Evaluator

The Fairy Godmother

Where would Cinderella be without her fairy godmother? This loving (though absentminded) magical fairy appears in Cinderella's life just when the girl has given up all hope for happiness. The Fairy Godmother waves her magic wand and says the magic words, and Cinderella's special night comes alive. She is the only one (except for Cinderella's animal friends, of course) who is kind to Cinderella in her time of need.

TRICKY TRIVIA

Q: What is the Fairy Godmother's signature magical phrase?

A: "Bibbidi-bobbidi-boo!"

The Fairy Godmother transforms a pumpkin into a beautiful carriage.

Finn McMissile

Finn McMissile is a master British spy. Though he's charming and eloquent, it's Finn's stealth maneuvering, intelligence, and years in the field that help him thwart bad guys and make daredevil escapes. Finn's prepared for any tricky situation with an arsenal of ultracool gadgets and weaponry, including front and rear grappling hooks, a missile launcher, deployable magnetic explosives, and a holographic disguise emitter.

COOL QUOTE

"My apologies, I haven't properly introduced myself. Finn McMissile, British intelligence."

Finn's on a mission!

Fix-It Felix, Jr.

Felix is the star of the video game *Fix-It Felix, Jr.* As Niceland's hammer-wielding maintenance man, Felix is beloved by all. He is hardwired for niceness, and anything other than being "The Good Guy" just doesn't compute. Eventually, Felix marries Calhoun and together they turn Niceland into a home for homeless video game characters, even adopting the orphaned *Sugar Rush* racers when that video game breaks down.

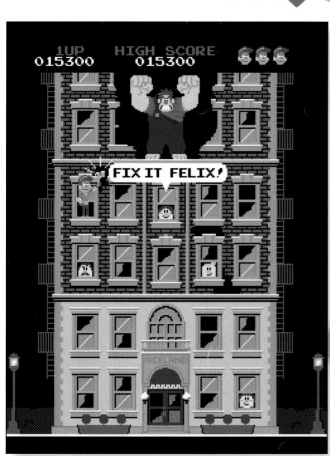

8-bit hero!

COOL QUOTE

"I can fix it!"

Flik

This goofy and brilliant worker ant is always getting his colony into deeper and deeper trouble. When he invents a machine to help the ants harvest grain faster, it only ends up knocking their entire collection of grain into the riverbed. This puts the ant colony in a terrible position when the bullying grasshoppers come to collect the grain. To make up for his mistake, Flik sets out to find some warrior bugs to help defend the ant colony against the mean grasshoppers. He unknowingly brings home a bunch of circus bugs instead. In the end, the circus bugs actually turn into heroes—as does Flik himself!

Flik is ready for adventure!

TRICKY TRIVIA

Q: How does Flik manage to fly away from Ant Island?

A: On a wispy dandelion seed

Flora, Fauna & Merryweather

These three good fairies are responsible for raising Princess Aurora until her sixteenth birthday. Hidden away in a forest cottage, the fairies' mission is to care for young Aurora and protect her from the evil fairy, Maleficent, and her wicked curse. They almost succeed, but then Maleficent tricks the princess into pricking her finger on a spinning wheel, triggering the terrible curse. The good fairies race to the rescue, helping Prince Phillip battle Maleficent by giving him the Shield of Virtue and the Sword of Truth. When Phillip triumphs over the evil fairy, the good fairies lead the brave prince to the Sleeping Beauty so his kiss can awaken her from her cursed sleep.

Living without magic is . . . challenging.

TRICKY TRIVIA

Q: What is Flora's favorite color?

A: Pink!

Q: What is Merryweather's favorite color?

A: Blue!

Flounder

Though he's sometimes reluctant to follow his more adventurous friend Ariel, Flounder always seems to be at the Little Mermaid's side, through thick and thin. He goes with her when she explores sunken ships—even when there are sharks lurking nearby. Later, he helps Ariel win her true love, Prince Eric. He even saves the day by helping Ariel swim to Prince Eric's ship, rescuing the prince and the entire undersea kingdom. Flounder is definitely a good friend to have in a tight spot!

COOL QUOTE

"I'm not a guppy!"

Being Ariel's friend sure gets Flounder into a lot of trouble!

Flynn

When Flynn Rider steals a crown from the kingdom of Corona, he has no idea it will change his life forever. While running from the palace guards, he hides in a tall tower—Rapunzel's tower to be exact. Rapunzel confronts Flynn and hides his stolen loot. She makes him agree to take her to see the floating lights outside the royal palace. Only then will she give him the crown back.

Flynn reluctantly agrees. But as he and Rapunzel adventure together, he finds he cares less and less about the crown, and more and more about Rapunzel. By the end of their journey, Flynn ends up sacrificing everything to save her from a life of captivity. Luckily for Flynn, that's not where the story ends. . . .

Flynn's famous "smolder"

COOL QUOTES

"Look, the only thing I want to do with your hair is get out of it! Literally!"

"Frying pans! Who knew, right?"

"They just can't get my nose right!"

Forky

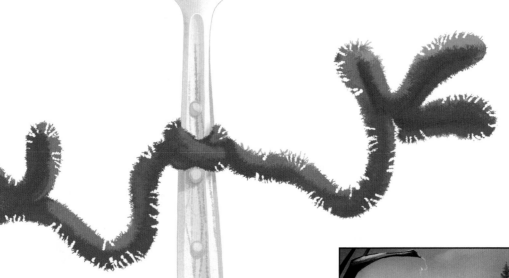

Forky is an adorable and spunky toy who was created by Bonnie on her very first day of kindergarten. Forky is filled with self-doubt—believing he is really trash and not a beloved toy—so he attempts to dive into any garbage can he passes. Eventually, after Woody saves Forky from the doll Gabby Gabby, he realizes that he's a valued toy and beloved friend to Bonnie and the rest of the gang.

COOL QUOTE

"I'm not a toy!"

Woody is doing his best to take Forky home to Bonnie.

Gaston

The arrogant bachelor Gaston wants nothing more than to marry Belle, but the bookish beauty has no interest in him . . . at all. This, of course, astounds Gaston. How could any young woman *not* want to marry a handsome, athletic hunter such as himself?

Though Gaston seems like nothing but a self-absorbed nuisance at first, his jealousy and rage take a dangerous turn, and he ends up leading an angry crowd of villagers to kill the Beast. (Luckily, the Beast battles back and, with some help from Belle, manages to defeat the villain.)

No one plots like Gaston.

NOT-SO-COOL QUOTE

"It's about time you got your head out of those books and paid attention to important things—like me."

The Genie

He's big. He's blue. And he's constantly changing. In fact, you never know quite what you're going to get with Aladdin's friend the Genie. He changes voices, characters, and even species! But you can usually tell who he is: he's the most outrageous personality in the room.

For thousands of years, the Genie dreamed of being free, but he never found a master who was willing to liberate him from the lamp. That is, until he met Aladdin. Instead of using his third wish for himself, Aladdin wishes the Genie free. Talk about true friendship!

FUN FACT

Comedian Robin Williams provided the voice of the Genie.

The Genie's powers include excellent fashion sense.

Geppetto

Geppetto the wood-carver lives a fairly ordinary life with his pet goldfish, Cleo, and his cat, Figaro. But when he makes a little wooden puppet and then wishes that the puppet be brought to life, Geppetto's life changes dramatically. The little wooden boy, of course, does come to life . . . and ends up causing poor Geppetto a lot of heartache before becoming a real boy at last.

Geppetto wishes on the Wishing Star.

COOL QUOTE

"Star light, star bright,
First star I see tonight.
I wish I may, I wish I might . . .
Have the wish I make tonight."

Goofy

Beloved by his friends, Goofy is fun-loving and . . . yes, goofy. But never fear—while Goofy may be somewhat clumsy, he is also kind, generous, shy, and unpredictable. He can easily bounce back from almost any predicament without a scratch. Goofy is good-natured and laid-back, and he's a great friend to both Mickey and Donald.

Under the deep blue sea

FUN FACT

The character we know as Goofy was originally called "Dippy Dawg."

Hercules

As the son of Zeus (the ruler of all the Greek gods), Hercules becomes a hero on earth. Raised by adoptive human parents, Hercules grows up an awkward and gawky boy. When he discovers that he is part god and part mortal, he goes into hero training. But his greatest test comes when the evil Hades drains Hercules of his godlike strength. Then Hercules must use true heroics to overcome the odds. He even saves all of the gods and goddesses as he defeats the wicked Hades. In the end, though, Hercules decides he would rather not become a god (though he has finally earned the right to join them). He would prefer to stay on earth with his one true (human) love, Meg.

Hercules the hero!

COOL QUOTE

"I want to become a hero, a true hero."

Holley Shiftwell

Holley Shiftwell is a young British desk agent turned spy-in-training. Well-educated and sharp, she knows every trick in the book—or rather, she relies on every trick in the spy manual. She's armed with all the latest state-of-the-art spy equipment imaginable, from hidden cameras and concealed weapons to a telescoping utility arm and a holographic pop-up display. Holley is a highly motivated agent, but she is fresh out of the academy, so her experience is based on lessons learned in school rather than in real-life situations. After she meets Mater, though, it isn't long before she learns to wing it.

TRICKY TRIVIA

Q: What is the name of the spy agency that Holley works for?

A: C.H.R.O.M.E. (That stands for "Command Headquarters for Recon Operations and Motorized Espionage.")

Holley is one high-tech agent!

Huey, Dewey & Louie

Huey, Dewey, and Louie are Donald Duck's inventive and dynamic nephews. These three little guys have a great sense of adventure and good fun. They have the strongest bond and are always vowing to do everything together. They are very brave, intelligent, and smart, and they love their uncle and their family. So, even after they've tangled Uncle Donald up in his hammock or played some practical joke on him, they usually end up back on Donald's good side.

Huey, Dewey, and Louie enjoy a rainy day.

DID YOU KNOW?

Here's how you can tell which nephew is which:

- Huey wears red. (Just remember that red is a nice, bright *hue*.)

- Dewey wears blue. (Think of *dew*, which is water, which sometimes looks blue.)

- Louie wears green. (*Louie* begins with the letter *L*, just like *leaves*, which are green!)

Ian Lightfoot

Ian Lightfoot is a sweet, soft-spoken elf who has always struggled with confidence. Although he has a loving family, Ian longs for the guidance and companionship of his father, who passed away before he was born. On Ian's sixteenth birthday, his life changes forever as he discovers something extraordinary about himself: he is a wizard! As he and Barley embark on a once-in-a-lifetime journey, Ian learns to loosen up and starts to see the world for all its messy but wonderful possibilities. And he begins to realize that there's more value in the things he already has than he might have thought.

Ian performs the Visitation Spell.

COOL QUOTE

"I was just wondering if you like parties because I was gonna do a party."

Jack-Jack

Jack-Jack is the odd man out in the Parr family—or is he? Although the only incredible thing he seems to be able to do is jabber in jibberish, he is actually a polymorph with an array of hidden powers. These powers are on full display when he takes on an intruding raccoon in the Parrs' backyard. Despite his many powers, Jack-Jack is a typical baby who makes mealtime messes and insists on having a full bottle and clean diaper, especially during story time with his dad.

FUN FACT

As Mr. Incredible says, Jack-Jack has seventeen powers—which is more powers than anyone else in his family!

Jack-Jack is still a baby, but his powers are Super.

Jaq & Gus

Two of Cinderella's best friends are mice who live in the walls of her stepfamily's house. Jaq and Gus love their friend Cinderella. She gives all her mouse friends clothes and food, and protects them from Lucifer, the cat. In return, the mice give her company when she's alone in her attic room. They even make her a dress for the ball! Later, they help free Cinderella from her locked room so that she can try on the glass slipper. When Cinderella moves into the palace to marry the Prince, she brings her mouse friends with her. After all, her happily ever after couldn't have happened without them!

Cinderella gives Gus a snazzy new shirt.

TRICKY TRIVIA

Q: What are the names of Cinderella's other mouse friends?

A: Bert, Luke, Mert, Perla, and Suzy

Jasmine

Born into royalty (she's the daughter of the Sultan), Jasmine is tough, smart . . . and a little bit lonely. Jasmine feels trapped in the palace and wants to be free to make her own choices. After sneaking out one day, she runs into a street rat named Aladdin. Jasmine likes him right away, but Aladdin feels that he'll never impress her in his rags.

When Aladdin comes to the palace as Prince Ali Ababwa, Jasmine thinks that Prince Ali is just like all her other stuck-up suitors. But then Prince Ali takes Jasmine on a magic carpet ride, and she begins to see that there's a kind and loving heart beneath his phony robes. After Jafar steals the magic lamp and reveals that Ali is really Aladdin, Jasmine feels betrayed. But Aladdin proves his courage by saving Jasmine and defeating the evil vizier. Her love for Aladdin is so strong that it convinces her father to change the law that requires her to marry a prince.

Aladdin shows Jasmine a whole new world.

TRICKY TRIVIA

Q: Who is Jasmine's best friend before she meets Aladdin?

A: Her pet tiger, Rajah

Jessie

When Woody is toy-napped by a greedy toy collector, he discovers that he was once the star of his own TV show, *Woody's Roundup*. One of his costars on the show was Jessie, the yodeling cowgirl. Woody meets Jessie in the collector's apartment, and the two begin a wonderful friendship.

Jessie tells Woody that he should live the life of a collectible toy because kids like Andy grow up—the way her owner did, eventually leaving Jessie behind. Woody decides to go back to Andy anyway, and he even brings Jessie home with him, where she learns to love and be loved once again by a real, live kid.

Jessie bonds with Andy's other toys right away—especially Buzz Lightyear. They spend many happy years together, and Andy eventually passes on all his toys to a little girl named Bonnie. Even though losing Andy is hard for Jessie and her friends, they know that Bonnie will take great care of them.

Jessie tells Woody about his early days as a cowboy star.

COOL QUOTES

"Sweet mother of Abraham Lincoln!"

"Oh, Bullseye, we're part of a family again!"

Jiminy Cricket

Little did Jiminy Cricket know what he was in for when he first entered Geppetto's workshop for a warm night's sleep. Soon after the cricket arrived, Geppetto finished carving a little wooden puppet named Pinocchio. That night, Pinocchio was brought to life by the Blue Fairy, who immediately assigned Jiminy the job of being Pinocchio's conscience. Jiminy and Pinocchio became good friends, and Jiminy was almost as excited as Geppetto when Pinocchio became a real boy.

Keeping Pinocchio out of trouble is a big job for a little cricket!

FUN FACT

As Pinocchio's conscience, Jiminy's official job title is Lord High Keeper of the Knowledge of Right and Wrong, Counselor in Moments of Temptation, and Guide Along the Straight and Narrow Path.

 Joy

Joy is one of our greatest emotions! Joy loves Riley more than anything and has been the little girl's lead Emotion since day one. She's lighthearted—a big fan of laughter, chocolate cake, and spinning until you get crazy dizzy and fall over. Hope and optimism dictate all of her decisions, and Joy works twice as hard as anyone else to accomplish her goals. She just wants Riley to be happy. After all, isn't that the point of life?

Joy tries to stop the Forgetters from taking away Riley's memories.

DID YOU KNOW?

Joy is the only Emotion in the film with a typical human name.

Judy Hopps

Judy Hopps is a little bunny with big dreams. A classic overachiever who is passionate about law enforcement and breaking down species barriers, Judy is the first bunny to join Zootopia's police department. Judy gets her chance to do some real police work when she manages to get herself assigned to find the missing Mr. Otterton. Judy is smart, fast, and sly. She easily outwits the sneaky Nick Wilde and convinces him to help her solve the case.

On her first day as a police officer, Judy writes a lot of tickets!

COOL QUOTES

"Sir, I am not just some token bunny!"

"You're gonna want to refrain from calling me 'Carrots.'"

Kristoff

Kristoff is a true outdoorsman. Rough around the edges, Kristoff's the strong, no-nonsense type who follows his own set of rules. He may seem like a loner, but he always has his best friends by his side: a loyal reindeer named Sven; a talking snowman named Olaf; Anna, the love of his life; and her sister, Elsa.

Some seem to think that Kristoff's being raised by trolls might make it difficult to communicate with the former ice harvester, but Anna doesn't mind; she has plenty to say for both of them. Kristoff loves being with his new family, whether they are playing charades during game night or they're off on some grand adventure.

Kristoff is sad. He was planning to propose marriage to Anna, but she left.

COOL QUOTE

"You know, under different circumstances, this would be a pretty romantic place . . . don't you think?"

Lady & Tramp

Lady isn't sure what to make of Tramp when he first comes into her well-groomed yard. Tramp is a mutt from the other side of town. He has no home and no family, unlike Lady, who lives with Jim Dear and Darling. However, after Tramp rescues Lady from the mean Aunt Sarah and then takes her to a romantic dinner at Tony's Restaurant, Lady finds herself falling in love. The two are a perfect match, and soon enough, Tramp comes to live in Lady's home for the rest of their happy lives together.

An unlikely pair

TRICKY TRIVIA

Q: What are the names of Aunt Sarah's cats?

A: Si and Am

Lady Tremaine

It is Cinderella's unfortunate fate that her father takes the cruel and wicked Lady Tremaine as his second wife. Along with her nasty daughters, Anastasia and Drizella, Lady Tremaine makes Cinderella a prisoner in her own home after her father's death. Condescending and rude, Lady Tremaine forces Cinderella to cook, clean, and wait on her and her daughters hand and foot.

Lady Tremaine locks Cinderella in her room to keep her from trying on the slipper.

DID YOU KNOW?

Lady Tremaine doesn't realize that Cinderella was at the ball until she overhears Cinderella humming the tune she danced to the night before. Lady Tremaine figures out that Cinderella is the girl the Prince is searching for.

Lightning McQueen

Poised to win the Piston Cup championship, Lightning McQueen has just two things on his mind: winning and the perks that come with it. But when he gets lost in the forgotten town of Radiator Springs and has to repave the main street (which he accidentally ruined), he's suddenly forced to rethink everything.

Thanks to the cars Lightning meets there, he soon discovers that friendship and teamwork are more important than winning and fame. (Though he still likes to win, of course!) In fact, Lightning goes on to compete in many races, including the World Grand Prix. But no matter how fast he goes, Lightning still loves slowing down with his friends in Radiator Springs.

Lightning zooms past his Italian rival, Francesco.

TRICKY TRIVIA

Q: Which historic highway is Radiator Springs located on?

A: Route 66

Q: The World Grand Prix takes place in which three countries?

A: Japan, Italy, and England

Lilo

When Lilo wishes on a falling star and asks for a friend, the little Hawaiian girl does not realize that the "falling star" is really a spaceship from the edges of the galaxy . . . and that it contains a genetic experiment gone wrong. Uh-oh. Soon Lilo adopts "Experiment 626," thinking the creature is a dog, and she names him Stitch. Over time, she teaches Stitch all about *'ohana*, and the little guy actually tosses aside his wild ways in order to become a part of Lilo's family.

Stitch's badness level is unusually high.

COOL QUOTES

"Dad said *'ohana* means family. Family means nobody gets left behind—or forgotten."

"I'm sorry I bit you. And pulled your hair. And punched you in the face."

"Stitch is troubled. He needs desserts."

Linguini

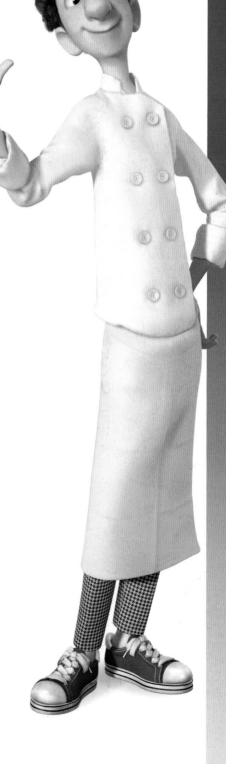

When Linguini first arrives at Gusteau's restaurant, he has no idea that he's really the long-lost son of the world-famous chef. All he wants is a simple job, but a chance encounter with a rat named Remy thrusts him into the gourmet spotlight. It turns out that Remy is a fantastic chef! Since Linguini can't cook at all, Remy gives him culinary instructions while hiding beneath Linguini's hat. Linguini soon finds himself the leader of the kitchen. But when Remy is discovered to be the true cooking genius, Linguini has a lot of explaining to do to his fellow chefs—and the health inspector!

Linguini takes notes in the kitchen.

TRICKY TRIVIA

Q: How does Remy control Linguini's actions in the kitchen?

A: By pulling his hair

The Lost Boys

In Never Land, Peter Pan lives inside the hollow Hangman's Tree along with the Lost Boys, a group of boys who hunt for treasure, battle pirates, and play games all day long. The Lost Boys love their fun lives, but sometimes—like when Wendy visits—they realize how much they miss having mothers. Still, when they are given the choice, they decide to stay in Never Land with their fearless leader, Peter Pan, instead of returning to London with Wendy, Michael, and John Darling.

John, Michael, and the Lost Boys go exploring.

TRICKY TRIVIA

Q: Can you name all the Lost Boys?

A: Cubby (dressed like a bear); Slightly (dressed like a fox); Nibs (dressed like a rabbit); the Twins (dressed like raccoons); and Tootles (dressed like a skunk)

The Mad Hatter

Alice meets the Mad Hatter as she searches Wonderland for the White Rabbit. The Mad Hatter and the March Hare are celebrating their unbirthdays with a beautiful tea party. But before Alice can drink any tea, the Mad Hatter insists that everyone trade seats. "Clean cups!" he shouts. Poor, confused Alice ends up leaving the tea party without drinking any tea! But a tea-less tea party is just the sort of silly thing the Mad Hatter loves.

The Mad Hatter "fixes" the White Rabbit's watch.

DID YOU KNOW?

The "10/6" label on the Mad Hatter's hat is actually a price tag. The 10 over the 6 means the hat would have cost ten shillings and sixpence.

Maid Marian

Maid Marian is King Richard's niece—and, therefore, pretty rich. You'd think that would make her and Robin Hood enemies, since he likes to rob from the rich and give to the poor. But the complete opposite is true—Marian is Robin Hood's one true love. When Marian and Robin were little, they were childhood sweethearts. Then, Marian moved to London, and the pair didn't see each other for many years. But when Robin and Marian meet up again in Nottingham, the two pick up right where they left off. Marian supports Robin Hood's cause fully and does whatever she can to help him defeat nasty Prince John.

Here comes the bride—and groom!

TRICKY TRIVIA

Q: When King Richard attends Marian's wedding to Robin Hood, what does he say?

A: "Now I have an outlaw for an in-law."

Maleficent

Enraged because she wasn't invited to Princess Aurora's birth celebration, the dark fairy Maleficent curses the new princess: "Before the sun sets on her sixteenth birthday, she shall prick her finger on the spindle of a spinning wheel and die!" After Maleficent hears that the three good fairies—Flora, Fauna, and Merryweather—have hidden the baby in order to save her, Maleficent spends the next sixteen years of her life searching for the princess. When at last the curse is fulfilled, Maleficent's happiness is short-lived. Merryweather was able to soften Maleficent's curse so that Aurora only falls into a deep sleep. Thanks to the good fairies and the brave Prince Phillip, the wicked sorceress is defeated, and Princess Aurora is awoken from the spell.

Maleficent transforms into a dragon to fight Phillip.

TRICKY TRIVIA

Q: Where is Maleficent's lair?

A: The Forbidden Mountains

Marie, Berlioz & Toulouse

These three little kittens belong to Madame Bonfamille, who spoils her felines and makes sure to encourage the little ones' talents. Marie, the only girl, is white and loves to sing. Toulouse is orange with a blue bow tie, and is usually ready for mischief. Berlioz is dark gray and is always picking fights with his siblings. Madame Bonfamille plans on leaving her entire (large) fortune to her cats. This, of course, makes her butler, Edgar, very jealous, and that's where the adventure begins!

COOL QUOTES

Marie: "Ladies do not start fights, but they can finish them!"

Toulouse: "You're not a lady!"

Berlioz: "You're nothing but a sister."

An evening outing

Marlin

This nervous clownfish suddenly turns into a hero when his only son, Nemo, is captured by a scuba diver. As soon as Nemo is scooped into the diver's bag, Marlin finds the courage he lost a long time ago. Facing sharks, a forest of jellyfish, and the whole of the wide-open sea, Marlin does not hesitate to do everything it takes to find Nemo. And when Marlin finally does find his son, no one is prouder of Marlin than Nemo himself.

Marlin and Dory go for a wild ride!

DID YOU KNOW?

When Marlin and Dory are stung by jellyfish, it doesn't hurt Marlin very much. Why? Because clownfish build up a slight immunity to stinging by living in their protective (and stinging) anemone homes.

Mater

Mater's a good ol' boy with a big heart, and he's the only tow truck in Radiator Springs. Mater runs Tow Mater Towing and Salvage and manages the local impound lot. Though a little rusty, he has the quickest towrope in Carburetor County and is always the first to lend a helping hand. Mater sees the bright side of any situation, and Radiator Springs wouldn't be the same without him. He doesn't have a mean bolt on his chassis. And when he meets up with some secret agents, he learns he's a natural at undercover work. There's nothing Mater can't do!

Mater learns he should go easy on the spicy wasabi.

TRICKY TRIVIA

Q: What color was Mater originally painted?

A: Light blue

Q: Mater claims that he is the world's best what?

A: Backward driver

Maui

In the past, Maui did many amazing things for humans, including bringing them fire and raising islands from the sea for them to live on. But Maui is also the reason that Motunui is dying. Eager to find bigger and better tasks to perform, Maui stole the heart of Te Fiti, the mother island, causing a darkness to spread that will gradually encompass the whole world. After a disastrous battle, Maui was marooned on a tiny island for a thousand years. His only companion was Mini Maui, a magical tattoo with a mind of its own—that is, until Moana lands on the island and gives him a chance to redeem himself.

The giant crab monster captures Moana!

COOL QUOTE

"I've got your back, chosen one.
Go save the world."

Maximus

Maximus is a royal guard horse who never lets criminals get away. When an adventurer named Flynn steals the lost princess's crown, Maximus is determined to find the thief. But when Maximus finally catches up to Flynn, he also meets Rapunzel. Rapunzel and Maximus quickly become friends, and Maximus reluctantly agrees (for Rapunzel's sake) not to arrest Flynn. That doesn't stop Maximus and Flynn from arguing all the time, though! During their entire journey, the two constantly tease each other. But when Rapunzel is in danger, these former enemies team up to help save the day . . . and Rapunzel!

FUN FACT

Maximus is one of the ring bearers at Flynn and Rapunzel's wedding.

Not exactly BFFs

Merida

Even though she's a princess, Merida is much more at home prowling through the forest than perched on a throne. Merida loves sword fighting and exploring the beautiful Scottish Highlands. She definitely takes after her father, King Fergus. Her greatest passion is archery—and she can aim an arrow better than anyone else! But her archery skills are completely lost on her mother, Queen Elinor, who sees a very different path for her daughter. Over time, Merida realizes that she has a little of both parents in her, and that she can be greater than the sum of those parts.

Bull's-eye!

COOL QUOTE

"There are those who say fate is something beyond our command. That destiny is not our own. But I know better. Our fate lives within us. You only have to be brave enough to see it."

Mickey Mouse

This little guy started it all for Walt Disney when he became the star of a number of Walt's earliest cartoons. First created as a mischievous rascal, Mickey has transformed over the years into an all-around nice guy. Sometimes shy, sometimes brave, and sometimes silly, Mickey is a dog's best friend (to Pluto) and sweetheart to Minnie Mouse. He loves adventure and trying new things, although his plans tend to go awry more often than not. Mickey usually appears in his signature red shorts, yellow shoes, and white gloves.

FUN FACT

Here are just a few of the jobs Mickey has held: firefighter, tailor, truck driver, pilot, storekeeper, detective, sorcerer's apprentice, and farmer.

Mickey and Pluto go fishing.

Miguel

Despite his family's baffling generations-old ban on music, Miguel Rivera dreams of becoming an accomplished musician like his idol, Ernesto de la Cruz. Desperate to prove his talent, Miguel finds himself in the colorful Land of the Dead following a mysterious chain of events. Along the way, he meets charming trickster Héctor, and together they set off on an extraordinary journey to unlock the real story behind Miguel's family history.

Héctor joins Miguel for a duet. They are a big hit.

FUN FACT

Miguel comes from the town of Santa Cecilia, named after the patron saint of music.

Mike Wazowski

Ever since he was a little monster, Mike knew he wanted to be a Scarer at Monsters, Inc. He studied hard, and even got into the Scare School at Monsters University. Eventually, Mike and his best friend, Sulley, work their way up from the Monsters, Inc., mail room to the Scare Floor. Everything seems to be going well, until a little human girl enters their lives, and Mike and Sulley must change the way they think about their world . . . from their status at Monsters, Inc., to the very way they collect energy for the city of Monstropolis. In the end, when the monsters discover they can collect more energy from children's laughter than from their screams, Mike really comes into his own. He's much better at making kids laugh than at scaring them!

FUN FACT

Monsters wear "odorant" to make themselves extra smelly. Some popular smells include Old Dumpster, Low Tide, and Wet Dog!

Mike's first day at Monsters University

Minnie Mouse

Minnie Mouse is Mickey's longtime girlfriend and best buddy. She can be very charming and gracious, a real lady who likes things that are elegant and fancy. But she is also very independent, talented, and dynamic—always ready for new adventures and ideas to try. Her best girl pal is Daisy Duck, and the two friends love to spend an afternoon together talking, shopping, and having a good time.

Minnie plays princess!

FUN FACT

Mickey and Minnie Mouse share the same birthday: November 18. This is the same day as the release of the first cartoon short in which they starred: *Steamboat Willie.*

Moana

Sixteen-year-old Moana has always felt drawn to the open ocean. She longs to explore the world beyond her island home of Motunui. But the people of Motunui are forbidden to travel past the reef, and as the daughter of the village chief, Moana has to set a good example for the villagers. When it becomes clear that her island is dying, she takes it upon herself to find a way to save Motunui. Moana is spirited and adventurous—when she feels strongly about something, she never gives up.

Moana, Maui, and Heihei are under attack!

FUN FACT

Moana's name means "ocean" in several Polynesian languages.

Mowgli

When Mowgli is just a baby, the panther Bagheera finds him abandoned in a broken boat. Bagheera takes the "Man-cub" to live with a family of wolves. The little boy grows up happy and carefree in the jungle . . . until the tiger Shere Khan begins to stalk him. It is then that Bagheera agrees to take the boy to a human village, where he rightfully belongs and can be protected from the wilds of the jungle. However, Mowgli doesn't want to leave the jungle, and he runs away, meeting up with a big, friendly bear named Baloo. After some wild adventures, Bagheera catches up with the pair, and Mowgli finally agrees to go to a village where he can live among humans like himself.

Oops!

COOL QUOTE

"I'll do anything to stay in the jungle!"

Mr. Incredible

Once the most famous Super alive, Mr. Incredible finds living life full time as Bob Parr, a mild-mannered insurance adjuster, more than a little unfulfilling. That's why when he gets the opportunity to don his suit once more he can't say no. Mr. Incredible battles a renegade robot on an uncharted island, and takes down the Super Villain, Syndrome (with a little help from his Super family). When Elastigirl leaves home for a special mission, Mr. Incredible must navigate day-to-day life with three busy kids— including baby Jack-Jack, whose superpowers are just starting to emerge!

Reading to Jack-Jack is exhausting for his Incredible dad.

COOL QUOTE

"No matter how many times you save the world, it always manages to get into jeopardy again."

Mrs. Potts & Chip

It's tough to be a teapot when you were once the bustling housekeeper of a castle (or a teacup, after having been a little boy). But Mrs. Potts and her son, Chip, make the best of it. They were transformed into enchanted objects, just like all the other castle servants, and they live in the cupboard with Chip's brothers and sisters. Mrs. Potts remains ever warm and friendly. Chip is always energetic, fun-loving, and inquisitive.

Chip always wants to stay up past his bedtime.

DID YOU KNOW?

Chip is the first enchanted object to see Belle. But no one believes that there's a girl in the castle until Lumiere and Babette see her, too!

Mufasa

Mufasa, the great Lion King, wants nothing more than to show his son, Simba, how to be a good ruler. He teaches Simba about bravery, the importance of protecting those around him, and the great Circle of Life. He also tells Simba about the kings of the past . . . and how they live in the stars above, watching over those who still live on Earth. After his father's death, Simba finds that these important lessons stay with him—no matter how hard he tries to run away from his responsibilities.

Later, Simba remembers his father's words when he takes over his rightful reign as king of the Pride Lands.

Mufasa and Sarabi welcome their new son.

COOL QUOTE

"Being brave doesn't mean you go looking for trouble."

Mulan

When her frail father is summoned to fight for the Chinese army, Mulan will do anything to save him—including dressing up as a man and joining the army in his place. But when the time comes to actually fight, she sees how difficult and dangerous her new job is. Using her quick wits, she manages to cause an avalanche that overcomes the enemy. But there's one problem: when she saves her captain, Li Shang, she is knocked unconscious. And when she awakens, she finds out that Shang knows she is a woman. Disgraced, Mulan is left behind by Shang and the rest of his army. But when she sees the leader of the enemy headed toward the Imperial City, she regains her courage and strength, and pursues him. In the end, she manages to save the Emperor himself . . . and bring pride and honor to her beloved family.

Mulan arrives at the army camp in disguise.

TRICKY TRIVIA

Q: What does Mulan call herself when she joins the army?

A: Ping

Q: What is the name of Mulan's dog?

A: Little Brother

Mushu

This fast-talking, troublemaking little dragon follows Mulan on her adventures in the army. He does it in order to save the Fa family name and regain his status as Fa family guardian. When Mulan first meets Mushu, she is startled to see that her ancestors have sent a little "lizard" to protect her. Nevertheless, Mushu does end up helping Mulan, even becoming one of her greatest allies in the final battle against Shan-Yu.

Mushu catches up on the news.

FUN FACT

Mushu seems to be the only one who understands Cri-Kee's speech. He often translates the little cricket's chirping.

Nala

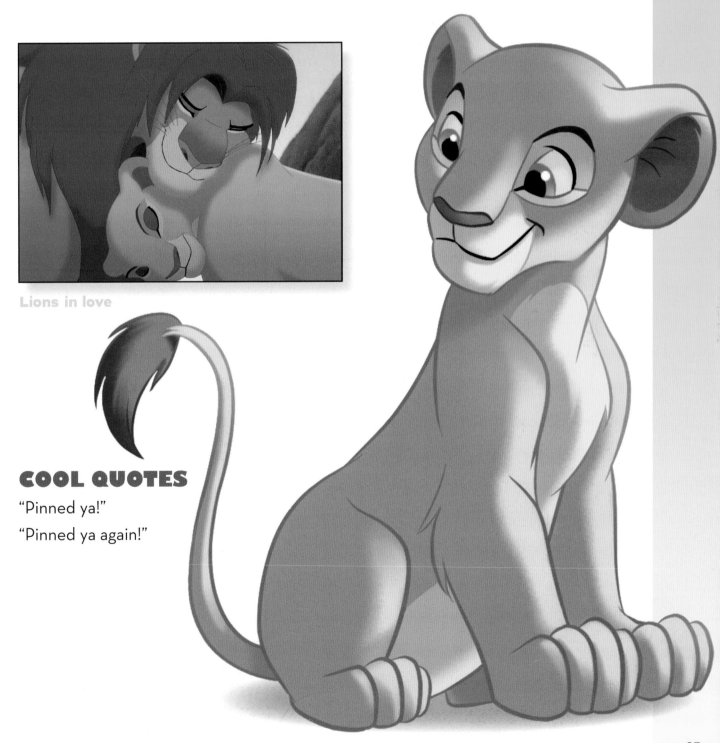

As Simba's first best friend, and later his mate, Nala is faithful to the end. She loves Simba for who he is, and she believes in his worth as the true king of the Pride Lands, even after he exiles himself for years. When Simba returns to face Scar, Nala follows him and helps him claim his place as king.

Lions in love

COOL QUOTES

"Pinned ya!"

"Pinned ya again!"

Naveen

Naveen is a prince from the faraway country of Maldonia. His love of jazz brings him to New Orleans to experience the toe-tapping music of the city. Naveen is never short on charm, but he's quite short on cash: his royal parents have stopped giving him any money until he learns a little responsibility. But instead of learning how to work for a living, Naveen turns to magic as a shortcut to wealth. That's when hardworking Tiana gets tangled up in the prince's problems, and the two are transformed into frogs! Only through his unlikely relationship with Tiana does Naveen grow up and discover an inner nobility he never knew he had.

Naveen thinks a kiss from Tiana will make him a prince again. Wrong!

FUN FACT

Naveen is the only Disney prince who doesn't have an American accent.

Nemo

Nemo is a little clownfish who lives a quiet life with his dad, Marlin, on the Great Barrier Reef. Nemo longs for adventure, but Marlin worries about the dangers of the ocean. Because one of Nemo's fins is small and weak, Marlin worries that he won't be able to take care of himself. One day, Nemo swims out into the open sea and is captured by a scuba diver. The diver puts Nemo in a fish tank where he meets a group of goofy new friends. Together, the friends figure out a way to escape the tank and Nemo is reunited with his dad. Nemo's little fin doesn't hold him back at all! Father and son return home, happy to be together again. And now Marlin knows that Nemo is ready for anything.

Nemo and the Tank Gang

TRICKY TRIVIA

Q: What nickname does the Tank Gang give Nemo?

A: Shark Bait

Nick Wilde

Nick has experienced contempt his whole life for being a fox; people assumed he was a "sly fox" con artist, so he decided to become one. He's charming, resourceful, and generally dishonest. That's why he and Judy Hopps don't get along at first. But Nick's resourcefulness allows him to find creative solutions, a trait that comes in handy when he and Judy team up to find the missing Mr. Otterton.

Nick Wilde is one clever fox, but he's met his match in Officer Hopps.

FUN FACT

Nick makes a cameo in *Big Hero 6*. His image appears on a billboard in San Fransokyo and on Honey Lemon's cell phone case.

Olaf

He's Olaf and he likes warm hugs. Created by Elsa's magical powers, Olaf is by far the friendliest snowman to walk the mountains above Arendelle. His innocence, outgoing personality, and uncanny ability to disassemble himself at good and not-so-good times lead to some awkward but hilarious moments. Olaf is absolutely fascinated with the wonders of life. On top of that, he has learned to read, and his questions have gotten bigger and more philosophical. He can also play a mean game of charades.

Olaf has never seen such a beautiful forest.

COOL QUOTE

"This will all make sense when I am older."

Oliver

At the beginning of *Oliver & Company*, a box of kittens is placed on a sidewalk in New York City, along with a sign reading KITTENS NEED HOME. Gradually, passersby adopt all the kittens—except for Oliver. Oliver has to fend for himself on the streets and eventually finds a home among some outcast dogs living on a barge with their down-and-out owner, Fagin. Later, a little girl named Jenny meets Oliver and offers him a loving home. Then he must decide between living with his adoptive dog family or with Jenny. In the end, Oliver decides to stay with Jenny, but his dog friends still come by to visit!

TRICKY TRIVIA

Q: Can you name all the dogs who live with Fagin on the barge?

A: Tito, Dodger, Einstein, Francis, and Rita

Dodger is always willing to lend a paw.

Pascal

Pascal is Rapunzel's oldest friend. Actually, he's her only friend until Rapunzel finally leaves her tower. At first, the little chameleon is a bit wary of Rapunzel's new companion, Flynn. He doesn't want Rapunzel to get hurt! But once he sees how happy Flynn makes Rapunzel, he warms up to the guy. And it's always easy to tell how Pascal feels about you—he changes color to match his mood!

Pascal loves to help Rapunzel.

FUN FACT

The opening scene of *Tangled* shows little Rapunzel in her royal crib. If you look closely, there's a small plush chameleon that looks just like Pascal on the princess's mobile!

Peter Pan

Peter Pan is a boy who will never, ever grow up. Luckily, he lives in Never Land, so remaining a child forever is actually possible. Peter loves living in Never Land, where he leads the Lost Boys on countless adventures, including going on treasure hunts, fighting pirates, meeting mermaids, and playing with a little fairy named Tinker Bell. He rarely ventures outside Never Land, but when he does, the real fun begins! It is one of his outside adventures that brings Wendy, Michael, and John Darling to Peter's world.

You can fly!

COOL QUOTE

"Second star to the right and straight on till morning."

Phillip

As a little boy, Prince Phillip attends a royal ceremony to welcome a neighboring princess into the world. His father promises his son's hand in marriage to the infant princess. Phillip and the princess grow up separately and meet one day by chance in the woods. There, they fall in love. Soon the princess falls under a wicked spell cast by the evil fairy Maleficent. But all is set right after Phillip escapes imprisonment and defeats Maleficent. Then Phillip is at last able to give True Love's Kiss to his Sleeping Beauty, breaking the spell forever.

The fairies enchant Phillip's sword.

TRICKY TRIVIA

Q: What are the two important things the good fairies give to Phillip to help him battle Maleficent?

A: The Shield of Virtue and the Sword of Truth

Q: What is the name of Prince Phillip's father?

A: King Hubert

Piglet

"The little pink guy" (as Tigger sometimes calls him) is one of the most faithful friends in the Hundred-Acre Wood, even though he's sometimes forgotten because of his size (which is very small). In fact, Piglet is so small that he could be swept away by a stiff breeze, along with the leaves he might be raking from his very neat front yard. An expert at baking haycorn pie and keeping his little house tidy, Piglet is a wonderful friend. And though he finds it hard to be brave, he always seems to gather the courage to help out a friend in need.

COOL QUOTES

"It's hard to be brave."

"Oh, d-d-d-dear!"

Falling leaves keep Piglet busy.

Pinocchio

After the Blue Fairy grants life to a puppet named Pinocchio, she promises to someday turn him into a real boy if he can prove himself brave, truthful, and unselfish. Unfortunately, even with the help of his conscience, Jiminy Cricket, Pinocchio finds it hard to always be good. He skips school to join a puppet show, lies to the Blue Fairy, and ends up in big trouble at Pleasure Island. But when Pinocchio risks his own life to save his father from a terrible whale—his first truly selfless act—he finally proves that he's worthy of becoming a real boy.

When Pinocchio lies, his nose grows!

COOL QUOTE

"I'm a real boy!"

Pluto

Pluto is Mickey Mouse's ever-faithful favorite pup. He is always very clear about his feelings. Friendly, loyal, and protective of Mickey Mouse, Pluto is also rather mischievous. When he gets into trouble, he "apologizes" by sheepishly putting his tail between his legs. But most of the time Pluto is a very good dog.

Mickey meets little Pluto in a pet shop.

COOL QUOTE

"Don't worry, Pluto. You're a better dog than any of them!"—Mickey Mouse

Pocahontas

Pocahontas loves the land where she grew up, from the waterfalls to the animals to the plants. In fact, one of her favorite advisers is Grandmother Willow, the spirit of a willow tree. When John Smith enters her life, Pocahontas discovers he shares her love of adventure and her desire to understand the unknown. Soon they find themselves becoming friends, despite the fact that their people are enemies. John Smith gets into trouble when trying to protect himself from a man in Pocahontas's tribe. Meanwhile, Governor Ratcliffe is trying to take over the land inhabited by Pocahontas's people, and he is willing to do anything to get his way. The brave Pocahontas throws herself in front of her own father's weapon to keep him from harming John Smith. She not only saves John Smith but also stops both of their peoples from starting a war neither will ever win.

Pocahontas enjoys the view.

TRICKY TRIVIA

Q: What is the name of the Powhatan warrior who wants to marry Pocahontas?

A: Kocoum

Pongo & Perdita

When Pongo the Dalmatian spots another lovely Dalmatian walking her human, he drags his man, Roger, to the park so they all can meet. It turns out the female human, Anita, is just as lovely as her dog. And soon Roger is falling in love with Anita, while Pongo courts Perdita. Later, the Dalmatian couple shares a double wedding with Roger and Anita, and Pongo and Perdita start a family that will rapidly grow to a total of 101 Dalmatians!

One big happy family!

TRICKY TRIVIA

Q: What is the puppies' favorite TV show?

A: *The Thunderbolt Adventure Hour*

Prince Charming

Prince Charming has never fallen in love . . . until Cinderella enters the ballroom, and the two dance the night away. Unfortunately, Cinderella has a curfew (which she strictly follows), and when she runs away at the stroke of midnight, the Prince is left with nothing to remember her by—nothing, that is, except a single glass slipper. That proves to be enough for the Prince to find his love and marry her . . . and live happily ever after.

One charming prince

TRICKY TRIVIA

Q: Which one of Cinderella's slippers does the Duke find on the palace steps?

A: Her left slipper

Quasimodo

It's a hard life being the Hunchback of Notre Dame, but Quasimodo makes the best of it. Though he has been held prisoner in the bell tower of Notre Dame cathedral most of his life, Quasimodo finds ways to make himself happy—by building little models of the people he sees far below the bell tower, and talking to his friends, the birds and the gargoyles. When he finally gets the chance to go outside the cathedral, he runs into more than his share of trouble. Still, he also finds new friends . . . and manages to open his life to love and trust.

Quasimodo and his new friends

TRICKY TRIVIA

Q: Who are Quasimodo's three gargoyle friends?

A: Hugo, Victor, and Laverne

Randall

Randall is one mean monster. His sharp teeth and chameleon-like ability to blend into his surroundings have made him the second-best Scarer at Monsters, Inc. But second best isn't good enough for this ambitious monster. He'll do whatever it takes to knock top Scarer Sulley out of the number one spot. Fortunately, Sulley and his buddy Mike are more than a match for Randall's evil schemes.

"Randy" wasn't always such a cool monster!

FUN FACT

Mike and Randall were roommates back in college at Monsters University.

111

Rapunzel

Rapunzel has been locked away in her tower for almost eighteen years. But she hasn't let those years go to waste! Rapunzel spends her time reading, cooking, and decorating her room with beautiful paintings. More than anything, Rapunzel wants to leave her tower and see the faraway floating lights for herself. But her strict caretaker, Mother Gothel, refuses to let her leave. See, Rapunzel has a secret— her hair is magical and can heal any wound! Mother Gothel claims that other people will hurt Rapunzel to use her hair. But with the help of her new friend, Flynn, Rapunzel leaves her tower and discovers that the outside world is a beautiful place. She also learns that she is really a princess, kidnapped by Mother Gothel as a baby! With this knowledge (and a little help from her friends), Rapunzel returns to her kingdom and takes her rightful place as princess.

Watch out for the frying pan!

FUN FACT

Rapunzel's hair is seventy feet long!

Remy

With a remarkable sense of smell and a genius for combining flavors, Remy is, without a doubt, like no other rat in France. He longs to be a chef like his idol, Auguste Gusteau, and not just a "poison sniffer" for his rat clan. When circumstances literally drop him into the kitchen of the great chef's restaurant, he finds himself living his dream of cooking (safely hidden from human eyes beneath his new friend Linguini's hat).

Remy smells something cooking!

COOL QUOTE

"I'm tired of taking. I want to make things. I want to add something to this world."

Rex

He may look like the most fearsome dinosaur in the toy box, but this tyrannosaurus is one of the most lovable toys of the bunch. Despite his endless worrying and insecurities about his quiet roar, Rex always comes through for his pals.

Rex is the scariest (and friendliest) dinosaur in Andy's room.

COOL QUOTES

"I don't like confrontations!"

"I can't look. Could somebody please cover my eyes?"

"Look at my little arms! I can't press the 'fire' button and jump at the same time!"

Riley Andersen

Riley Andersen is a cheerful eleven-year-old girl with a spirited imagination. She has a quiet confidence and is charmingly awkward. But her confidence is shaken when her family moves from Minnesota to San Francisco. Struggling to adjust to a new city and make new friends, Riley's happy-go-lucky personality begins to fade. Fortunately, the Emotions are able to help her through it all and she ends up thriving in her new home.

Joy loves remembering how happy Riley was when she skated on ice.

FUN FACT

Riley appears to be ambidextrous. She is shown as a toddler drawing Bing Bong on the wall with her left hand. She uses her right hand when she is eating.

Robin Hood

Who steals from the rich and gives to the poor? Robin Hood, of course! He takes care of England—and her less fortunate citizens— when the king leaves the country in the hands of his selfish brother, Prince John. It's clear Robin's on the right side when he grabs rubies from the greedy John and delivers food and toys to the poor children of the land. His childhood sweetheart, Maid Marian, is so impressed, she falls in love with him all over again!

Robin makes his escape!

TRICKY TRIVIA

Q: What are Robin's helpers called?

A: The Merry Men

Q: How does Robin disguise himself at the archery tournament?

A: He dresses up like a stork.

Sadness

Sadness has always been a "glass half empty" kind of Emotion. She'd love to be more optimistic, but it's hard to stay positive when the world's so full of misery. Sometimes Riley faces challenges in her life, and Sadness has no choice but to collapse in a puddle of sorrow, "turn on the waterworks," and signal Mom and Dad for help. It's a painful job, but Sadness perseveres, one agonizing day at a time.

Joy draws a Circle of Sadness.

FUN FACT

Sadness's appearance is based on a teardrop.

Sally

Sally grew tired of her life in the fast lane as a high-powered attorney in Los Angeles, so she made a new start in the small town of Radiator Springs. Charming, intelligent, and witty, she became the town attorney. She also became the car most dedicated to preserving the town's historical beauty. She even bought a motel and restored it to its original condition, and she doesn't plan to stop there. She'd fix the town building by building if that's what it took.

Sally shows Lightning around beautiful Carburetor County.

TRICKY TRIVIA

Q: What is Sally's nickname for Lightning?
A: Stickers

Scar

It's bad news for Scar when Simba is born. Simba is the son and rightful heir of the Lion King, Mufasa, which means his Uncle Scar is no longer next in line for the crown. However, it doesn't take Scar long to put an evil plan into place—by luring Simba into a thundering stampede. When Mufasa finds out Simba is in danger, he leaps to his son's rescue. Mufasa dies, and Simba feels terribly sad and guilty. Scar encourages him to run away. Unfortunately for Scar, however, Simba is the one and only true Lion King. And when he returns to take over his rightful role, the evil Scar meets his end at last.

Scar and Mufasa do not see eye to eye.

TRICKY TRIVIA

Q: What are the names of the three hyenas who help Scar?

A: Shenzi, Banzai, and Ed

Scuttle

Scuttle the seagull has his own special way of thinking about things. Ariel and the others see him as a sort of expert on human items, but it's pretty clear he isn't very knowledgeable at all. Upon seeing a fork, he labels it a "dinglehopper" and says, "Humans use these little babies to straighten their hair out." Scuttle may not be wise, but he certainly is creative!

COOL QUOTES

"Well, look at what the catfish dragged in!"

"Have I ever been wrong? I mean when it's *important*!"

Scuttle tells Ariel all about "dinglehoppers."

Sebastian

Sebastian is the court composer for King Triton's undersea kingdom. That means the crab is also Ariel's singing coach. When Ariel gets into trouble with her father, the blustery King Triton tells Sebastian to look after the Little Mermaid and keep her safe. Sebastian fails miserably in his quest to keep Ariel from danger (and humans), but he soon becomes Ariel's greatest helper in winning the heart of Prince Eric. And when Ariel gets into real trouble with the sea witch, Ursula, Sebastian stands by her to the end.

Sebastian knows Ariel is up to something!

TRICKY TRIVIA

Q: What is Sebastian's full name?

A: Horatio Felonious Ignacious Crustaceous Sebastian

The Seven Dwarfs

Each of the Dwarfs has his own unique personality, but they all agree on one thing—their love for Snow White. **Doc** is the leader of the Seven Dwarfs (at least in his own mind). With glasses and a bumbling manner of speech, he stands out from the rest. **Grumpy** certainly lives up to his name. But sometimes (like when Snow White kisses him on the forehead), you can catch a glimmer of a smile on his face. **Dopey** never speaks, but he does have a voice. He also has endearingly large ears and a wide grin. **Sleepy** (*yawn!*) has a very difficult time staying awake. **Happy** is, well, happy. And like the other Dwarfs, he races quite seriously to Snow White's rescue when the wicked Queen gives her the poisoned apple. **Sneezy** suffers from a hopeless case of hay fever . . . and anything else that can possibly make a fellow sneeze. **Bashful**, as Walt Disney once said, is secretly in love with Snow White. Of course, this makes his blushing even worse than normal, especially when she kisses him good-bye.

TRICKY TRIVIA

Q: What do the Seven Dwarfs mine?

A: Diamonds

The Dwarfs are surprised by their visitor.

Simba

Simba grows up living the life of a carefree prince. He believes he deserves to get whatever he wants because he is the future Lion King. But when his father is tragically killed, Simba thinks the death is his fault. Sad and torn with guilt, he runs away from his destiny. He grows up in a desert oasis with his friends, Timon and Pumbaa, ignoring his role as the king of the Pride Lands. Later, after some encouragement from his childhood friend Nala, Simba realizes it is time to return home. There he battles his evil Uncle Scar and takes his rightful place as the Lion King at last.

COOL QUOTES

"I just can't wait to be king!"

"I finally got some sense knocked into me. And I've got the bump to prove it."

"You're Mufasa's boy."

Snow White

Though she is royal by birth, Snow White is forced into a role of servitude as the wicked Queen's scullery maid. She dreams, however, of finding her one true love. The Prince actually does meet her at her wishing well as she is fetching water, but it is not until the end of the film that she gets her first kiss from him— Love's First Kiss. That kiss, of course, breaks the evil spell put upon Snow White by the vain Queen. Snow White's sweet and gentle nature makes her beloved by all. Even before her happy ending, Snow White is befriended by the forest animals—and of course the Seven Dwarfs!

Happily ever after

FUN FACT

Snow White and the Seven Dwarfs was the first film to issue a soundtrack album.

Stitch

Formerly known as alien Experiment 626, Stitch accidentally ends up on Earth when he tries to escape being sent to a distant asteroid prison. He lands in Hawaii, where he is mistaken for a dog, adopted by a little girl named Lilo, and given a new name and a new life. There he learns all about *'ohana* ("family") and gradually progresses from being a naughty alien bent on destruction to being a caring member of Lilo's family.

Stitch sure knows how to make a mess!

TRICKY TRIVIA

Q: Why doesn't Stitch like water when he first lands on Earth?

A: He can't swim!

Sulley

Sulley may look like a friendly, furry blue guy covered in purple spots, but if he popped out of your closet in the middle of the night, he'd look downright scary! In fact, Sulley comes from a family of famous Scarers, attended Scare School like his dad, and was then named top Scarer at Monsters, Inc., a full thirty-six months in a row. Then a little girl named Boo escaped into Monstropolis and changed his life forever. Now Sulley collects laughs instead of screams!

"Mikey, there's a scream shortage. We're walking."

TRICKY TRIVIA

Q: What is Sulley's full name?

A: James P. Sullivan

Sven

A reindeer with the heart of a Labrador, Sven is Kristoff's loyal friend, sleigh puller, and conscience. He makes sure his ice-harvester companion is the stand-up guy Sven knows and loves, and does so without saying a word. A few emphatic snorts usually get his point across. Although Kristoff now has the love of his life, he still finds himself leaning on Sven to help him deal with his emotions. Sven's heroism shows us (once again) why reindeer are better than people.

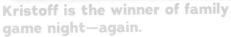
Kristoff is the winner of family game night—again.

FUN FACT

Kristoff found Sven as a baby. Sven was abandoned, injured, and starving until Kristoff saved the little reindeer's life and nursed him back to health. The two have been inseparable ever since!

Thumper

One of Bambi's first and best friends, Thumper is a curious, exuberant, and sometimes overly talkative bunny. He's the one who shows the young prince around the forest when Bambi is just a few hours old, and continues to be his constant companion.

Thumper thumps for Bambi and Flower.

COOL QUOTE

"I'm thumpin'! That's why they call me Thumper!"

Tiana

Tiana is one hard worker! Her dream is to one day open her very own New Orleans restaurant. Inspired by her father, she knows everything about cooking and running a business, but there are still some pretty big obstacles standing in the way of her dream. She works multiple waitress jobs (with no time for romance!), saving every penny she can.

All of Tiana's efforts are interrupted, however, when she meets the irresponsible Prince Naveen. His foolish choices have gotten him turned into a frog. And when Tiana tries to help him, she gets turned into a frog, too! The unlikely couple has to work together to break the spell, and along the way, Tiana learns to open herself up to love.

Once she's human again, Tiana does achieve her dream of opening a restaurant. And with Naveen at her side, Tiana realizes she has not only everything she *wants*, but also all that she *needs*.

Tiana learned to cook when she was just a little girl.

COOL QUOTE

"Daddy never got what he wanted . . . but he had what he needed: love! He never gave that up, and neither will I!"

Tigger

"**H**oo-hoo-hoo! Bouncin's what tiggers do best!" Well, actually, flying kites, playing Pooh Sticks, planting seeds, building houses, having parties, eating cake, and a number of other things are also what tiggers do best (according to Tigger, that is). Tigger is very proud of himself and his unique status of being the "onliest tigger." He is Roo's best friend and hero, and together the two have a jolly time bouncing and playing throughout the Hundred-Acre Wood, despite Rabbit's frequent angry protests.

Tigger just loves to bounce!

COOL QUOTES

"A watched pot never spoils!"

"Look both ways before bossing!"

"A friend in need is a friend who needs ya."

Timon & Pumbaa

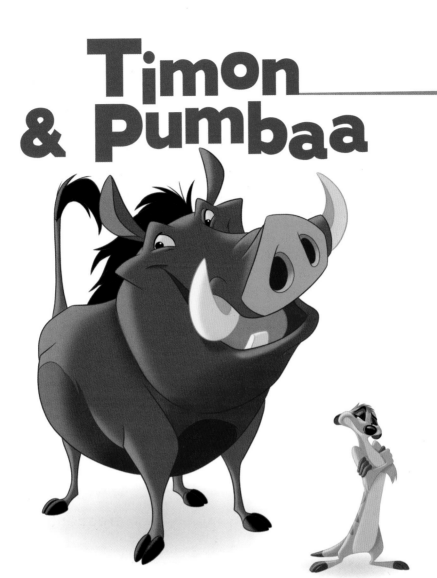

Timon and Pumbaa not only saved Simba's life, they also taught him to be happy again. Their motto, *"hakuna matata,"* means "no worries." And that's just how the two friends live their lives—worry free.

During the time he spent with the meerkat and warthog, Simba grew from a cub to a full-grown lion. And when the time came for him to return to the Pride Lands and claim his rightful place as king, Simba was ready, thanks to his two pals.

Pumbaa's got himself in a tight spot!

COOL QUOTES

Pumbaa: "It's times like this my buddy Timon here says, 'You got to put your behind in your past.'"

Timon: "No, no, no. It's 'You got to put your past behind you.'"

Timothy Mouse

Who says elephants are afraid of mice? Timothy Mouse becomes Dumbo's best pal, helping the baby elephant through the tough times that follow his separation from his mother. And when Dumbo learns to fly, it's Timothy who gives him the confidence he needs to realize he can fly on his own.

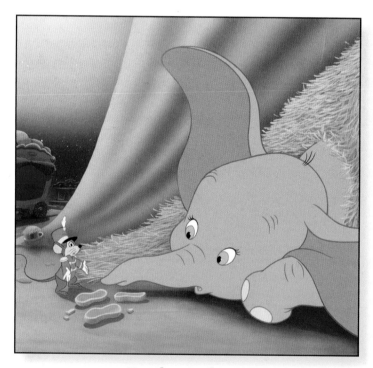

"Look, Dumbo—I'm your friend!"

DID YOU KNOW?

Timothy's middle initial is Q. That's Timothy Q. Mouse.

Tinker Bell

Smart, fast, and capable, Tinker Bell is Peter Pan's sidekick. She is coquettish, pouting, jealous, and spiteful but also caring and protective when it comes to Peter. Tink sends word to the Lost Boys to shoot down the "Wendy Bird" that is on the way to Peter's hideout, and she's later punished for her jealous nature when Peter sends her away. Tricked by Hook, Tink does everything she can to save Peter before it's too late. Tink speaks only in jingles, which the residents of Never Land are able to understand.

Tinker Bell is jealous of Wendy. She wants her to go home.

DID YOU KNOW?

In 2010, Tinker Bell was honored with a star on the Hollywood Walk of Fame.

Ursula

Ursula the sea witch had vowed to get revenge on Ariel's father, King Triton, ever since he banished her from the kingdom of Atlantica. So when she discovered that Ariel had fallen in love with a human prince named Eric, she quickly seized her chance. She made a deal with the mermaid to make Ariel human for three days, in exchange for the mermaid's voice. If Ariel received the Kiss of True Love by then, she could be a human forever. If not, she would join the other poor merpeople who'd lost their souls in Ursula's "garden."

Bad idea, Ariel.

TRICKY TRIVIA

Q: What are the names of Ursula's eel henchmen?

A: Flotsam and Jetsam

Q: What does Ursula keep Ariel's voice in?

A: Her shell necklace

Vanellope

Known as a "glitch," Vanellope believes she is a programming mistake in the candy-coated racing game *Sugar Rush*. With a racer's spirit embedded in her coding, Vanellope is determined to earn her place in the starting lineup among the other racers. The only problem: the other racers don't want her or her glitching in the game. When *Sugar Rush* breaks down, Vanellope and Ralph travel to the Internet to try to get the game fixed. Vanellope eventually finds the game she was meant to play and says a heartfelt good-bye to Ralph (although they plan to visit each other).

Vanellope loves the Internet. Ralph finds it very confusing!

COOL QUOTE

"We're gonna do it, Ralph. We're actually going to save my game."

135

WALL•E

WALL•E is programmed to clean up the hopelessly polluted planet Earth, one trash cube at a time. However, after seven hundred years, he's the only working robot left on Earth, and he's developed quite a personality. He's extremely curious and a little lonely—and it's really no surprise that when the lovely robot named EVE appears, WALL•E instantly falls in love. But he never could have imagined how big an adventure they would have together.

WALL•E is crazy about EVE.

DID YOU KNOW?

WALL•E stands for Waste Allocation Load Lifter, Earth class.

Wendy, John & Michael Darling

Even before they travel to Never Land, Wendy, John, and Michael Darling know all about Peter Pan. That's because of the stories they have been told about him. When Peter actually does enter their bedroom one night in search of his lost shadow, the three children readily agree to return with him to Never Land for a true adventure. So with a sprinkling of magic pixie dust from Tinker Bell (along with some happy thoughts), Wendy, Michael, and John are soon able to fly . . . all the way to Never Land.

Time isn't the only thing that flies with Peter Pan!

TRICKY TRIVIA

Q: What is the name of the Darling children's dog?

A: Nana

137

The White Rabbit

He's late. He's very, very late. In fact, he always seems to be late. That's the White Rabbit. When he first runs past Alice with his giant watch, he declares that he is quite tardy. Curious, Alice follows him all the way to Wonderland, where her adventures begin. In fact, if it weren't for the White Rabbit, Alice would never have made it to Wonderland.

FUN FACT
In the film, every time the White Rabbit looks at his watch, the time is 12:25.

"I'm late!"

The Wicked Queen

The vain Queen consults her Magic Mirror regularly to assure herself that she is the most beautiful in the land. One day, when the Magic Mirror honestly answers that the young maiden Snow White is fast becoming more beautiful, the wicked Queen decides to get rid of her. Luckily, Snow White is able to escape to the cottage of the Seven Dwarfs. The Queen eventually finds the princess there, and uses her magic powers to transform herself into an old peddler woman to trick Snow White into eating a poisoned apple. But even the disguise and the magic are not enough to keep Snow White from her true love. The Queen finally meets a bad end: when the Seven Dwarfs chase her to the top of a mountain, lightning strikes the rock she is on, and she tumbles down, never to be seen again.

"This is no ordinary apple. It's a magic wishing apple."

COOL QUOTE

"Magic Mirror on the wall,
who is the fairest one of all?"

Winnie the Pooh

This much beloved bear of very little brain seems always to be in search of honey. He adores his smackerels of the sticky yellow stuff and will do just about anything to have some, including getting stuck in beehives, putting himself in danger of being stung, and overstuffing himself! Pooh's best friend is Christopher Robin, but he's also quite close to his little pal Piglet, as well as everybody else in the Hundred-Acre Wood. In fact, everybody seems to love Pooh.

Pooh will do anything for honey!

FUN FACT

Pooh once ate so much of Rabbit's honey that he couldn't fit through the door of his friend's house afterward.

Woody

Woody is at the top of the toy chain in Andy's room—until Andy gets a Buzz Lightyear toy for his birthday. With Buzz's arrival, Woody's status as favorite toy is threatened—and his role as leader of the toys is also placed in jeopardy. Soon, however, Woody learns to overcome his jealousy in favor of friendship, and he risks everything to save Buzz from Andy's toy-destroying neighbor, Sid. Later, Buzz returns the favor by saving his toy-napped pal from the scheming toy collector Al McWhiggin.

Woody has been through a lot as Andy's toy, but the hardest thing of all was saying good-bye to Andy when he left for college years later. Luckily, Andy left all his toys with Bonnie, an imaginative young girl who will take great care of everyone. Eventually, Woody leaves Bonnie's house to join Bo Peep out in the real world so they can help other kids and toys.

Woody rides with daredevil Duke Caboom.

FUN FACT

Officially, Woody's last name is "Pride," although that name has never appeared in any of the Toy Story films.

Wreck-It Ralph

Ralph is a big guy with an even bigger heart. For thirty years, he has dutifully done his job as the Bad Guy in the arcade game *Fix-It Felix, Jr.* But it gets harder and harder to love his job when no one seems to like him for doing it. He eventually proves that he's not such a bad guy, and travels to the Internet with his best friend, Vanellope, to make sure her *Sugar Rush* game gets fixed. Even though Ralph and Vanellope end up going their separate ways, Ralph has already proved what a loyal and caring friend he is.

Ralph and Vanellope travel through the information superhighway.

COOL QUOTES

"I'm gonna wreck it!"

"Whiffee? Wifey? It's either Wiffle ball or an arranged marriage game."

Zazu

Zazu is Mufasa's nervous steward. He does everything from reporting on the news in the Pride Lands to babysitting Simba and Nala. Later, when Scar becomes king, Zazu continues as royal steward, but he has to do so from his cage-like prison next to Scar. Nobody is happier than Zazu when Simba returns to take his place as the rightful king of the Pride Lands.

TRICKY TRIVIA

Q: What kind of bird is Zazu?
A: A hornbill

Zazu tries to protect Simba and Nala.

List of Characters